THE BR...
TREASURES
IN FOCUS

Magna Carta

MAGNA CARTA is one of the most celebrated documents in English history but later interpretations have tended to obscure its real significance in 1215. The charter was a practical solution to a political crisis. It primarily served the interests of the barons by limiting unjust and arbitrary behaviour by the king. The charter contained few statements of legal principle and very little of it dealt directly with the villeins, the unfree peasantry, who formed the majority of the population. It failed to secure lasting peace in 1215 and only three clauses are still valid today, but the longevity and adaptability of a few key clauses have secured its iconic status. Above all, it established the critical principle that the king, like his people, was subject to the law.

King John's reign was dominated by a prolonged struggle with the Church, disastrous military campaigns in France and a rebellion by many of the English barons which culminated in the granting of Magna Carta.

John's conflict with the Church was rooted in a complex dispute over the election of a new archbishop of Canterbury. This dispute led to years of deadlock between John and Pope Innocent III. Finally in 1213, when threatened with growing baronial opposition and the prospect of a French invasion, John surrendered England to the feudal overlordship of the papacy, turning his enemy, the pope, into his ally overnight.

The barons' grievances stemmed from John's costly but largely unsuccessful attempts to defend the vast English empire in France. To finance his military campaigns, John exploited his feudal rights beyond all customary limits, demanding extortionately high taxes, exacting punitive fines and seizing baronial estates. He dealt with rebels by disregarding justice, taking hostages and imposing ruthless punishments.

The barons sought a charter of liberties to defend themselves against the king, but John resisted pressure to negotiate. He eventually agreed to meet his opponents who set out their demands in the document known as the Articles of the Barons.

On 10 June 1215 negotiations between King John and the rebel barons began at Runnymede by the River Thames. The demands listed in the Articles of the Barons were revised and new clauses were added, until finally the terms of Magna Carta were agreed. The precise detail and timing of events are uncertain, but by 19 June an oral settlement had been made, the barons had renewed their homage to the king and all parties had sworn an oath to observe the agreement.

Following the meeting, scribes from the royal chancery wrote up the terms agreed at Runnymede into the formal royal grant subsequently known as Magna Carta, which is Latin for the Great Charter. Many copies of this grant were issued but only four now survive, one each in Lincoln and Salisbury and two at the British Library. There is no evidence that a single original copy of Magna Carta was drawn up and ceremonially sealed during the meeting at Runnymede.

Although King John had agreed to the terms of Magna Carta, he was confident that Pope Innocent

III, his feudal overlord since 1213, would never agree to the charter's restrictions on his royal authority. In July 1215 John sent envoys to the pope seeking an annulment of the charter and, before most of its terms could be properly implemented, Innocent III issued a papal bull on 24 August 1215 declaring Magna Carta null and void. It had been legally valid for only ten weeks.

Within months, civil war had broken out in England, but in October 1216 King John died suddenly and was succeeded by his nine-year-old son, Henry III. William Marshal, the regent, sought to convert moderate barons to the young king's cause by reissuing Magna Carta with substantial revisions in both 1216 and 1217. Henry III issued his own further revised version in 1225. This version was repeatedly confirmed by medieval kings and was added to the statute roll as Edward I's 1297 confirmation of the 1225 text.

The majority of the sixty-three clauses in Magna Carta deal not with broad legal principles and rights but with the regulation of feudal customs and the operation of the justice system. King John's extortionate exploitation of his feudal rights and his ruthless administration of justice were at the core of the barons' grievances. As well as strongly reflecting these baronial complaints, Magna Carta also has clauses on towns and trade, the extent and regulation of the royal forest, debt, the Church and practical measures for the restoration of peace. Some clauses specifically include all free men in their remit, but very few relate to the mass of the unfree peasantry.

The most radical clause set up an elected commision of twenty-five barons to monitor and enforce the king's compliance with the charter. The commission could seize the king's lands to force him to rectify any failure to adhere to the settlement. This consolidated the limitations on the authority and autonomy of the king inherent in Magna Carta.

Magna Carta was handwritten by royal scribes in Latin, the language of government and record in King John's England. The scribes wrote the charter with quill pens on sheets of parchment made from treated sheepskin, the usual writing surface of the period. Because parchment was very expensive to produce, the scribes used a small script and abbreviated the Latin text to save space. Each of the surviving copies of Magna Carta is a different size and shape, and each has minor textual variations, but none is more authoritative than the others.

In common with other medieval royal charters, Magna Carta was authenticated with the great seal, not the king's signature. The double-sided design of the great seal was applied to a mixture of beeswax and resin and attached to the foot of the charter with plaited cords. Only one of the four surviving copies of Magna Carta retains a trace of its original seal.

Although only four copies of Magna Carta survive, the issue of thirteen is recorded and many more were probably produced since the king had ordered a public proclamation of the charter. Copies were sent to bishops, sheriffs and other officials throughout England and the text was read out locally in translation.

Only three of the original clauses in Magna Carta are still legally valid. One defends the freedom and rights of the English Church, another confirms the liberties and customs of London and other towns, but the third is the most famous:

> No free man shall be seized or imprisoned, or stripped of his rights or possessions, or outlawed or exiled … nor will we proceed with force against him … except by the lawful judgement of his equals or by the law of the land. To no one will we sell, to no one deny or delay right or justice.

This statement of principle, buried deep in Magna Carta, was given no particular prominence in 1215. It applied only to the free men of England, but its intrinsic adaptability has allowed succeeding generations to reinterpret it for their own purposes and this has ensured its longevity. In the fourteenth century, Parliament saw it as guaranteeing trial by jury. Sir Edward Coke, the Chief Justice, interpreted it as a declaration of individual liberty in his conflict with the early Stuart kings. It has resonant echoes in the American Bill of Rights and the Universal Declaration of Human Rights. Even today, it is regularly cited by lawyers and quoted by politicians for their own ends.

But the real legacy of Magna Carta as a whole is that it limited the king's authority by establishing the crucial principle that the law was a power in its own right to which the king, like his people, was subject.

Clauses marked (+) are still valid under the charter of 1225, but with a few minor amendments. Clauses marked (*) were omitted in all later reissues of the charter. In the charter itself the clauses are not numbered, and the text reads continuously. The translation sets out to convey the sense rather than the precise wording of the original Latin.

JOHN, by the grace of God King of England, Lord of Ireland, Duke of Normandy and Aquitaine, and Count of Anjou, to his archbishops, bishops, abbots, earls, barons, justices, foresters, sheriffs, stewards, servants, and to all his officials and loyal subjects, Greeting.

KNOW THAT BEFORE GOD, for the health of our soul and those of our ancestors and heirs, to the honour of God, the exaltation of the holy Church, and the better ordering of our kingdom, at the advice of our reverend fathers Stephen, archbishop of Canterbury, primate of all England, and cardinal of the holy Roman Church, Henry archbishop of Dublin, William Bishop of London, Peter bishop of Winchester, Jocelin bishop of Bath and Glastonbury, Hugh bishop of Lincoln, Walter bishop of Worcester, William bishop of Coventry, Benedict bishop of Rochester, Master Pandulf subdeacon and member of the papal household, Brother Aymeric master of the knighthood of the Temple in England, William Marshal earl of Pembroke, William earl of Salisbury, William earl of Warren, William earl of Arundel,

Alan de Galloway
constable of Scotland,
Warin Fitz Gerald, Peter
Fitz Herbert, Hubert de
Burgh seneschal of Poitou,
Hugh de Neville, Matthew
Fitz Herbert, Thomas
Basset, Alan Basset,
Philip Daubeny, Robert
de Roppeley, John Marshal,
John Fitz Hugh, and
other loyal subjects:

+ (1) FIRST, THAT WE
HAVE GRANTED TO
GOD, and by this present
charter have confirmed for
us and our heirs in
perpetuity, that the English
Church shall be free, and
shall have its rights
undiminished, and its
liberties unimpaired.
That we wish this so to
be observed, appears from
the fact that of our own
free will, before the
outbreak of the present
dispute between us and
our barons, we granted
and confirmed by charter

the freedom of the
Church's elections – a
right reckoned to be of
the greatest necessity and
importance to it – and
caused this to be
confirmed by Pope
Innocent III. This freedom
we shall observe ourselves,
and desire to be observed
in good faith by our heirs
in perpetuity.

TO ALL FREE MEN OF
OUR KINGDOM we have
also granted, for us and
our heirs for ever, all the
liberties written out below,
to have and to keep for
them and their heirs, of
us and our heirs:

(2) If any earl, baron, or
other person that holds
lands directly of the
Crown, for military
service, shall die, and at
his death his heir shall
be of full age and owe a
'relief', the heir shall
have his inheritance on

payment of the ancient scale of 'relief'. That is to say, the heir or heirs of an earl shall pay £100 for the entire earl's barony, the heir or heirs of a knight 100s. at most for the entire knight's 'fee', and any man that owes less shall pay less, in accordance with the ancient usage of 'fees'.

(3) But if the heir of such a person is under age and a ward, when he comes of age he shall have his inheritance without 'relief' or fine.

(4) The guardian of the land of an heir who is under age shall take from it only reasonable revenues, customary dues, and feudal services. He shall do this without destruction or damage to men or property. If we have given the guardianship of the land to a sheriff, or to any person

answerable to us for the revenues, and he commits destruction or damage, we will exact compensation from him, and the land shall be entrusted to two worthy and prudent men of the same 'fee', who shall be answerable to us for the revenues, or to the person to whom we have assigned them. If we have given or sold to anyone the guardianship of such land, and he causes destruction or damage, he shall lose the guardianship of it, and it shall be handed over to two worthy and prudent men of the same 'fee', who shall be similarly answerable to us.

(5) For so long as a guardian has guardianship of such land, he shall maintain the houses, parks, fish preserves, ponds, mills, and everything else pertaining to it, from the revenues of

the land itself. When the heir comes of age, he shall restore the whole land to him, stocked with plough teams and such implements of husbandry as the season demands and the revenues from the land can reasonably bear.

(6) Heirs may be given in marriage, but not to someone of lower social standing. Before a marriage takes place, it shall be made known to the heir's next-of-kin.

(7) At her husband's death, a widow may have her marriage portion and inheritance at once and without trouble. She shall pay nothing for her dower, marriage portion, or any inheritance that she and her husband held jointly on the day of his death. She may remain in her husband's house for forty days after his death, and within this period her dower shall be assigned to her.

(8) No widow shall be compelled to marry, so long as she wishes to remain without a husband. But she must give security that she will not marry without royal consent, if she holds her lands of the Crown, or without the consent of whatever other lord she may hold them of.

(9) Neither we nor our officials will seize any land or rent in payment of a debt, so long as the debtor has movable goods sufficient to discharge the debt. A debtor's sureties shall not be distrained upon so long as the debtor himself can discharge his debt. If, for lack of means, the debtor is unable to discharge his debt, his sureties shall be answerable for it. If they so desire, they may have

the debtor's lands and rents until they have received satisfaction for the debt that they paid for him, unless the debtor can show that he has settled his obligations to them.

* (10) If anyone who has borrowed a sum of money from Jews dies before the debt has been repaid, his heir shall pay no interest on the debt for so long as he remains under age, irrespective of whom he holds his lands. If such a debt falls into the hands of the Crown, it will take nothing except the principal sum specified in the bond.

* (11) If a man dies owing money to Jews, his wife may have her dower and pay nothing towards the debt from it. If he leaves children that are under age, their needs may also be provided for on a scale appropriate to the size of his holding of lands. The debt is to be paid out of the residue, reserving the service due to his feudal lords. Debts owed to persons other than Jews are to be dealt with similarly.

* (12) No 'scutage' or 'aid' may be levied in our kingdom without its general consent, unless it is for the ransom of our person, to make our eldest son a knight, and (once) to marry our eldest daughter. For these purposes only a reasonable 'aid' may be levied. 'Aids' from the city of London are to be treated similarly.

+ (13) The city of London shall enjoy all its ancient liberties and free customs, both by land and by water. We also will and grant that all other cities, boroughs, towns, and ports shall enjoy all their liberties and free customs.

* (14) To obtain the general consent of the realm for the assessment of an 'aid' – except in the three cases specified above – or a 'scutage', we will cause the archbishops, bishops, abbots, earls, and greater barons to be summoned individually by letter. To those who hold lands directly of us we will cause a general summons to be issued, through the sheriffs and other officials, to come together on a fixed day (of which at least forty days notice shall be given) and at a fixed place. In all letters of summons, the cause of the summons will be stated. When a summons has been issued, the business appointed for the day shall go forward in accordance with the resolution of those present, even if not all those who were summoned have appeared.

* (15) In future we will allow no one to levy an 'aid' from his free men, except to ransom his person, to make his eldest son a knight, and (once) to marry his eldest daughter. For these purposes only a reasonable 'aid' may be levied.

(16) No man shall be forced to perform more service for a knight's 'fee', or other free holding of land, than is due from it.

(17) Ordinary lawsuits shall not follow the royal court around, but shall be held in a fixed place.

(18) Inquests of *novel disseisin, mort d'ancestor,* and *darrein presentment* shall be taken only in their proper county court. We ourselves, or in our

absence abroad our chief justice, will send two justices to each county four times a year, and these justices, with four knights of the county elected by the county itself, shall hold the assizes in the county court, on the day and in the place where the court meets.

(19) If any assizes cannot be taken on the day of the county court, as many knights and freeholders shall afterwards remain behind, of those who have attended the court, as will suffice for the administration of justice, having regard to the volume of business to be done.

(20) For a trivial offence, a free man shall be fined only in proportion to the degree of his offence, and for a serious offence correspondingly, but not so heavily as to deprive him of his livelihood. In the same way, a merchant shall be spared his merchandise, and a villein the implements of his husbandry, if they fall upon the mercy of a royal court. None of these fines shall be imposed except by the assessment on oath of reputable men of the neighbourhood.

(21) Earls and barons shall be fined only by their equals, and in proportion to the gravity of their offence.

(22) A fine imposed upon the lay property of a clerk in holy orders shall be assessed upon the same principles, without reference to the value of his ecclesiastical benefice.

(23) No town or person shall be forced to build bridges over rivers except those with an ancient obligation to do so.

(24) No sheriff, constable, coroners, or other royal officials are to hold lawsuits that should be held by the royal justices.

* (25) Every county, hundred, wapentake, and riding shall remain at its ancient rent, without increase, except the royal demesne manors.

(26) If at the death of a man who holds a lay 'fee' of the Crown, a sheriff or royal official produces royal letters patent of summons for a debt due to the Crown, it shall be lawful for them to seize and list movable goods found in the lay 'fee' of the dead man to the value of the debt, as assessed by worthy men. Nothing shall be removed until the whole debt is paid, when the residue shall be given over to the executors to carry out the dead man's will. If no debt is due to the Crown, all the movable goods shall be regarded as the property of the dead man, except the reasonable shares of his wife and children.

* (27) If a free man dies intestate, his movable goods are to be distributed by his next-of-kin and friends, under the supervision of the Church. The rights of his debtors are to be preserved.

(28) No constable or other royal official shall take corn or other movable goods from any man without immediate payment, unless the seller voluntarily offers postponement of this.

(29) No constable may compel a knight to pay money for castle-guard if the knight is willing to undertake the guard in

person, or with reasonable excuse to supply some other fit man to do it. A knight taken or sent on military service shall be excused from castle-guard for the period of this service.

(30) No sheriff, royal official, or other person shall take horses or carts for transport from any free man, without his consent.

(31) Neither we nor any royal official will take wood for our castle, or for any other purpose, without the consent of the owner.

(32) We will not keep the lands of people convicted of felony in our hand for longer than a year and a day, after which they shall be returned to the lords of the 'fees' concerned.

(33) All fish-weirs shall be removed from the Thames, the Medway, and throughout the whole of England, except on the sea coast.

(34) The writ called *precipe* shall not in future be issued to anyone in respect of any holding of land, if a free man could thereby be deprived of the right of trial in his own lord's court.

(35) There shall be standard measures of wine, ale, and corn (the London quarter), throughout the kingdom. There shall also be a standard width of dyed cloth, russet, and haberject, namely two ells within the selvedges. Weights are to be standardised similarly.

(36) In future nothing shall be paid or accepted for the issue of a writ of

inquisition of life or limbs. It shall be given *gratis*, and not refused.

(37) If a man holds land of the Crown by 'fee-farm', 'socage', or 'burgage', and also holds land of someone else for knight's service, we will not have guardianship of his heir, nor of the land that belongs to the other person's 'fee', by virtue of the 'fee-farm', 'socage', or 'burgage', unless the 'fee-farm' owes knight's service. We will not have the guardianship of a man's heir, or of land that he holds of someone else, by reason of any small property that he may hold of the Crown for a service of knives, arrows, or the like.

(38) In future no official shall place a man on trial upon his own unsupported statement, without producing credible witnesses to the truth of it.

+ (39) No free man shall be seized or imprisoned, or stripped of his rights or possessions, or outlawed or exiled, or deprived of his standing in any other way, nor will we proceed with force against him, or send others to do so, except by the lawful judgement of his equals or by the law of the land.

+ (40) To no one will we sell, to no one deny or delay right or justice.

(41) All merchants may enter or leave England unharmed and without fear, and may stay or travel within it, by land or water, for purposes of trade, free from all illegal exactions, in accordance with ancient and lawful customs. This, however, does not apply in time of war to merchants

from a country that is at war with us. Any such merchants found in our country at the outbreak of war shall be detained without injury to their persons or property, until we or our chief justice have discovered how our own merchants are being treated in the country at war with us. If our own merchants are safe they shall be safe too.

* (42) In future it shall be lawful for any man to leave and return to our kingdom unharmed and without fear, by land or water, preserving his allegiance to us, except in time of war, for some short period, for the common benefit of the realm. People that have been imprisoned or outlawed in accordance with the law of the land, people from a country that is at war with us, and merchants – who shall be

dealt with as stated above – are excepted from this provision.

(43) If a man holds lands of any 'escheat' such as the 'honour' of Wallingford, Nottingham, Boulogne, Lancaster, or of other 'escheats' in our hand that are baronies, at his death his heir shall give us only the 'relief' and service that he would have made to the baron, had the barony been in the baron's hand. We will hold the 'escheat' in the same manner as the baron held it.

(44) People who live outside the forest need not in future appear before the royal justices of the forest in answer to general summonses, unless they are actually involved in proceedings or are sureties for someone who has been seized for a forest offence.

* (45) We will appoint as justices, constables, sheriffs, or other officials, only men that know the law of the realm and are minded to keep it well.

(46) All barons who have founded abbeys, and have charters of English kings or ancient tenure as evidence of this, may have guardianship of them when there is no abbot, as is their due.

(47) All forests that have been created in our reign shall at once be disafforested. River-banks that have been enclosed in our reign shall be treated similarly.

* (48) All evil customs relating to forests and warrens, foresters, warreners, sheriffs and their servants, or river-banks and their wardens, are at once to be investigated in every county by twelve sworn knights of the county, and within forty days of their enquiry the evil customs are to be abolished completely and irrevocably. But we, or our chief justice if we are not in England, are first to be informed.

* (49) We will at once return all hostages and charters delivered up to us by Englishmen as security for peace or for loyal service.

* (50) We will remove completely from their offices the kinsmen of Gerard de Athée, and in future they shall hold no offices in England. The people in question are Engelard de Cigogné, Peter, Guy, and Andrew de Chanceaux, Guy de Cigogné, Geoffrey de Martigny and his brothers, Philip Marc and his

brothers, with Geoffrey his nephew, and all their followers.

* (51) As soon as peace is restored, we will remove from the kingdom all the foreign knights, bowmen, their attendants, and the mercenaries that have come to it, to its harm, with horses and arms.

* (52) To any man whom we have deprived or dispossessed of lands, castles, liberties, or rights, without the lawful judgement of his equals, we will at once restore these. In cases of dispute the matter shall be resolved by the judgement of the twenty-five barons referred to below in the clause for securing the peace. In cases, however, where a man was deprived or dispossessed of something without the lawful judgement of his equals by

our father King Henry or our brother King Richard, and it remains in our hands or is held by others under our warranty, we shall have respite for the period commonly allowed to Crusaders, unless a lawsuit had been begun, or an enquiry had been made at our order, before we took the Cross as a Crusader. On our return from the Crusade, or if we abandon it, we will at once render justice in full.

* (53) We shall have similar respite in rendering justice in connexion with forests that are to be disafforested, or to remain forests, when these were first afforested by our father Henry or our brother Richard; with the guardianship of lands in another person's 'fee', when we have hitherto had this by virtue of a 'fee' held of us for knight's service by a third party; and with abbeys

founded in another person's 'fee', in which the lord of the 'fee' claims to own a right. On our return from the Crusade, or if we abandon it, we will at once do full justice to complaints about these matters.

(54) No one shall be arrested or imprisoned on the appeal of a woman for the death of any person except her husband.

* (55) All fines that have been given to us unjustly and against the law of the land, and all fines that we have exacted unjustly, shall be entirely remitted or the matter decided by a majority judgement of the twenty-five barons referred to below in the clause for securing the peace together with Stephen, archbishop of Canterbury, if he can be present, and such others as he wishes to bring with him. If the archbishop cannot be present, proceedings shall continue without him, provided that if any of the twenty-five barons has been involved in a similar suit himself, his judgement shall be set aside, and someone else chosen and sworn in his place, as a substitute for the single occasion, by the rest of the twenty-five.

(56) If we have deprived or dispossessed any Welshmen of lands, liberties, or anything else in England or in Wales, without the lawful judgement of their equals, these are at once to be returned to them. A dispute on this point shall be determined in the Marches by the judgement of equals. English law shall apply to holdings of land in England, Welsh law to those in Wales, and the law of the Marches to

those in the Marches. The Welsh shall treat us and ours in the same way.

* (57) In cases where a Welshman was deprived or dispossessed of anything, without the lawful judgement of his equals, by our father King Henry or our brother King Richard, and it remains in our hands or is held by others under our warranty, we shall have respite for the period commonly allowed to Crusaders, unless a lawsuit had been begun, or an enquiry had been made at our order, before we took the Cross as a Crusader. But on our return from the Crusade, or if we abandon it, we will at once do full justice according to the laws of Wales and the said regions.

* (58) We will at once return the son of Llywelyn, all Welsh hostages, and the charters delivered to us as security for the peace.

* (59) With regard to the return of the sisters and hostages of Alexander, king of Scotland, his liberties and his rights, we will treat him in the same way as our other barons of England, unless it appears from the charters that we hold from his father William, formerly king of Scotland, that he should be treated otherwise. This matter shall be resolved by the judgement of his equals in our court.

(60) All these customs and liberties that we have granted shall be observed in our kingdom in so far as concerns our own relations with our subjects. Let all men of our kingdom, whether clergy or laymen, observe them similarly in their relations with their own men.

* (61) SINCE WE HAVE GRANTED ALL THESE THINGS for God, for the better ordering of our kingdom, and to allay the discord that has arisen between us and our barons, and since we desire that they shall be enjoyed in their entirety, with lasting strength, for ever, we give and grant to the barons the following security:

The barons shall elect twenty-five of their number to keep, and cause to be observed with all their might, the peace and liberties granted and confirmed to them by this charter.

If we, our chief justice, our officials, or any of our servants offend in any respect against any man, or transgress any of the articles of the peace or of this security, and the offence is made known to four of the said twenty-five barons, they shall come to us – or in our absence from the kingdom to the chief justice – to declare it and claim immediate redress. If we, or in our absence abroad the chief justice, make no redress within forty days, reckoning from the day on which the offence was declared to us or to him, the four barons shall refer the matter to the rest of the twenty-five barons, who may distrain upon and assail us in every way possible, with the support of the whole community of the land, by seizing our castles, lands, possessions, or anything else saving only our own person and those of the queen and our children, until they have secured such redress as they have determined upon. Having secured the redress, they may then resume their normal obedience to us.

Any man who so desires may take an oath to obey the commands of the twenty-five barons for the achievement of these ends, and to join with them in assailing us to the utmost of his power. We give public and free permission to take this oath to any man who so desires, and at no time will we prohibit any man from taking it. Indeed, we will compel any of our subjects who are unwilling to take it to swear it at our command.

If one of the twenty-five barons dies or leaves the country, or is prevented in any other way from discharging his duties, the rest of them shall choose another baron in his place, at their discretion, who shall be duly sworn in as they were.

In the event of disagreement among the twenty-five barons on any matter referred to them for decision, the verdict of the majority present shall have the same validity as a unanimous verdict of the whole twenty-five, whether these were all present or some of those summoned were unwilling or unable to appear.

The twenty-five barons shall swear to obey all the above articles faithfully, and shall cause them to be obeyed by others to the best of their power.
We will not seek to procure from anyone, either by our own efforts or those of a third party, anything by which any part of these concessions or liberties might be revoked or diminished. Should such a thing be procured, it shall be null and void and we will at no time make use of it, either ourselves or through a third party.

* (62) We have remitted and pardoned fully to all men any ill-will, hurt, or grudges that have arisen between us and our subjects, whether clergy or laymen, since the beginning of the dispute. We have in addition remitted fully, and for our own part have also pardoned, to all clergy and laymen any offences committed as a result of the said dispute between Easter in the sixteenth year of our reign (i.e. 1215) and the restoration of peace.

In addition we have caused letters patent to be made for the barons, bearing witness to this security and to the concessions set out above, over the seals of Stephen archbishop of Canterbury, Henry archbishop of Dublin, the other bishops named above, and Master Pandulf.

* (63) IT IS ACCORDINGLY OUR WISH AND COMMAND that the English Church shall be free, and that men in our kingdom shall have and keep all these liberties, rights, and concessions, well and peaceably in their fullness and entirety for them and their heirs, of us and our heirs, in all things and all places for ever.

Both we and the barons have sworn that all this shall be observed in good faith and without deceit. Witness the above-mentioned people and many others.

Given by our hand in the meadow that is called Runnymede, between Windsor and Staines, on the fifteenth day of June in the seventeenth year of our reign (i.e. 1215: the new regnal year began on 28 May).

All images are taken from BL Cotton Augustus ii.106

First published 2007 by
The British Library
96 Euston Road
London
NW1 2DB

British Library Cataloguing in Publication Data
A catalogue record for this book is available from
The British Library

ISBN 978-0-7123-0965-3

Designed and typeset in Berkeley by Bobby & Co, London
Colour reproductions by Dot Gradations Ltd, UK
Printed in China by Great Wall Printing